fast thinking: proposal

PEARSON EDUCATION LIMITED

Head Office:
Edinburgh Gate
Harlow CM20 2JE
Tel: +44 (0)1279 623623
Fax: +44 (0)1279 431059

London Office:
128 Long Acre
London WC2E 9AN
Tel: +44 (0)20 7447 2000
Fax: +44 (0)20 7240 5771
Website: www.business-minds.com

First published in Great Britain in 2001

© Pearson Education Limited 2001

The right of Ros Jay to be identified as Author
of this Work has been asserted by her in accordance
with the Copyright, Designs and Patents Act 1988.

ISBN 0 273 65312 1

British Library Cataloguing in Publication Data
A CIP catalogue record for this book can be obtained from the British Library

10 9 8 7 6 5 4 3 2 1

Typeset by Pantek Arts Ltd, Maidstone, Kent.
Printed and bound in Great Britain by Ashford Colour Press, Hampshire.

The Publishers' policy is to use paper manufactured from sustainable forests.

fast
thinking:
proposal

▶ **make your case**

▶ **write with flair**

▶ **get a result**

by Ros Jay

contents

introduction

You've got a proposal to write … yesterday. Well, today just about scrapes through but that's as far as you can push it. Someone important – your boss, your MD, a key customer – is expecting it on their desk by tomorrow. Obviously you *should* have started on it sooner, but there's always so much other work piling up, and then there's that awful sinking feeling you get whenever you think about writing proposals. It does nothing to galvanize you into action.

Now, however, the clock is going to galvanize you. Panic has risen to the point where you can't ignore it any longer and you just *have* to get on with the damn thing. But how? Part of the problem, I suspect, is that you're not sure how best to go about it – certainly not in the time you've got left. This proposal is important. It could make or break a sale or a business loan from the bank, or influence top management's opinion of you. What if it's no good? What if it doesn't convince them?

It's a funny thing, but no one ever teaches us how to write proposals. It's not part of the training.

We get sent on courses to teach us everything from time management to maternity legislation – but proposal writing always gets left out. And yet it is a central management skill. We all have to do it, apparently without any help.

Well, the panic's over. This book will take you only an hour to read, and it will tell you everything you need to know to write a truly impressive and convincing proposal. No waffle, no unnecessary background – you haven't got time for all that. Just the essentials (but all of them, mind).

Of course it's better to have more time, and this book also tells you what to do with it when you *do* have it (next time …). But what you need right now is the fast thinker's version. You want:

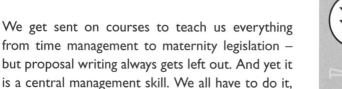 **tips for looking as if you know more than you do**

shortcuts for doing as little preparation as possible

checklists to run through at the last minute

… all put together clearly and simply. And short enough to read fast, of course.

This book will tell you how to write a proposal in a day. Yes, it can be done – no sweat. In fact, at the end of the book, you'll find guidelines for writing a proposal in an evening if you're cutting things really fine. And if you like to sail truly close to the wind, there's even a one-hour version. So if it can be done in an hour, doing it in a day should be a breeze.

So relax, put the answerphone on, and don't panic. Everything you need to know is in here, and it will get you through the preparation in as little as an hour if that's all you've got. But the longer, the better. Any additional time you have over an hour is a bonus, so if you have a whole evening to write your proposal ... you've got time to make yourself a cup of coffee before you even start.

This book will take you through the seven key stages of preparing and writing a proposal:

1 To begin with, you'll need to set your objective. This makes everything that comes after it more effective.

2 Next, you'll need to collect together all the information you want to include – at least everything you can collect in the time.

3 Now you need to work out what order you're going to say everything in – in other words you have to give your proposal a structure.

4 Many people find the most daunting aspect of proposals is the actual writing bit. So we'll look at how to write in a clear, readable style which will get your point across.

5 The mechanics of writing English can be as fraught as the style, so the next chapter will fill you in on everything from vocab to punctuation.

6 However clear the structure, and however slick the writing, your proposal will let you down if it doesn't look good. So this is the next stage – presentation.

7 Finally, you need to finish off the proposal with summaries, appendices and all that stuff – so we'll run through everything you need to know about topping and tailing.

fast thinking
gambles

If you can write a proposal in a day, or even an hour, what is the point of trying to make more time to do the job? Why not learn to do it in, say, an evening every time? That is certainly an option, but it's not the best one. The thing is that fast thinking will achieve your objective – to produce a convincing and professionally presented proposal – but it still has its limitations. When you limit your time, you limit your options.

And while you certainly want to be fast, you also want to be the best. After all, many managers can date the start of their success to a particular proposal which was admired higher up the organization. So what are the drawbacks of proposal writing at breakneck speed?

- For arguments to be convincing, they must be backed up by hard facts. So you have to research all the facts you need to support your case. You cannot lay your hands on as much information in an hour as you can in a couple of days. And suppose you can only get the data you need from someone else, and they are out of the office until next week?

- If you find the writing part tough, you're not going to find it gets any easier with the sword of Damocles hanging over you. It's one thing to find a good way of expressing what you want to say; quite another to find the *best* way.

- Although a proposal should rarely be very long, there is often enough information in there that the typing alone takes a fair while. When you're really under pressure, you may have to leave out information that would have been better included.

- The presentation of your proposal is hugely influential – you know what they say about first impressions. With more time, you can put finishing touches to your proposal which you simply can't find time for this time around. For example, it can look far smarter to retype data for an appendix in the style of your proposal rather than attach photocopies of figures or pages from other documents.

- It's always a good idea to get someone else – or several someone elses – to read through an important proposal before you submit it. The tighter the time, the harder it is to fit in this important stage.

1 your objective

What's your objective? You may be thinking, 'To get this proposal written as fast as possible – that's what!' Well, that's a perfectly good objective. But the proposal itself also needs a clear objective. Like every activity, large or small, you have a far better chance of achieving your aim quickly and effectively if you know exactly what that aim is.

The more thinking you do at the start of the process of writing a proposal, the less work you will have to do later. Honest. And that's why you need to begin with a clear objective. Once you have a clear objective you can:

- **see easily what information to include in your proposal**
- **see easily what information to omit**
- **be consistent in content and style throughout the proposal.**

GET IT IN WRITING

Make yourself write down a clear objective before you start, following the guidelines here. It should take five minutes at the most. Then prop it up on the desk in front of you the whole time you're working on the proposal.

So your proposal will be focused and clear in its intent, and therefore far more likely to persuade the reader of your point of view. And you won't waste time researching or writing information which doesn't need to be there.

GETTING THE PITCH

To begin with, your objective should help you to pitch your proposal accurately at the people it is intended for. This makes a big difference. Think of it in a different context for a moment. Suppose you are trying to persuade two of your friends to go on a surfing holiday in Hawaii with you. One is adventurous, the other a lover of creature comforts. You would use very different arguments to propose the same holiday.

The more thinking you do at the start of the process of writing a proposal, the less work you will have to do later

Selling adventure	Selling comfort
Great surfing beaches	Stay in a luxury hotel
Plenty of other water sports on offer	Laze on the beach in the sunshine
Exciting and unusual location	Spend the evenings eating out at open air restaurants

So you can see that you need to know the person – or people – you are writing your proposal for in order to pitch it as persuasively as possible. To do this, you should begin by asking yourself:

- ▸ **Who is the proposal for?**

- ▸ **What is their level of knowledge on the subject?**

- ▸ **What will they use the proposal for (persuading someone else, justifying the cost, making a straight yes/no decision)?**

- ▸ **What aspects do they particularly want covered (costs, staffing, technical problems, logistics and so on)?**

- ▸ **What does the proposal *not* need to cover (technical details, justifications of cost when money isn't an issue etc.)?**

This thought process should take you only a few moments, but will help hugely in setting a clear objective. Suppose you are proposing to your board that staffing levels in your department be increased. A statement of your aim might be simply that: To persuade the board to increase staffing levels in the department. But the more detail you add, the more helpful your objective will be. That means it will save you time and increase the chance of your proposal being accepted.

Compare it to a journey. Imagine you're in London and you want to go to New York. You could head off vaguely in a westerly direction and start asking the way somewhere around Cardiff. You might find a boat heading for the USA and when you arrived you could start hitching. I expect you'd get there eventually.

But that isn't what most of us do. We establish the best way to get there before we start. A way that doesn't only get us to New York, but does it comfortably, quickly, economically and according to any other requirements we have.

The same holds for writing your proposal. You need to decide not only where you are going, but also what the main requirements of your route are, and what aspects of the subject you want to visit on the way. So the objective needs to be fleshed out a little. Here's a fresh version: To persuade the board that increased staffing levels in the department would be more productive.

You need to decide not only where you are going, but also what the main requirements of your route are

Now we're getting somewhere. But we need to be still more specific. What does 'more productive' mean? More cost-effective? Or will it generate more income? Or speed up the system? What benefit are you trying to sell to your board? What turns them on? Cutting costs? Increasing output? Improving customer service? Operating a faster system?

OK, let's try again: To persuade the board that increased staffing levels in the department would improve customer service and generate more

THIRD TIME LUCKY

It often takes three stages to set a clear objective. Identify the broad objective first, then state a broad reason why your reader should accept it, and finally make the reason more specific. For example:

1 persuade the board to up staffing levels

2 to make the department more productive

3 in terms of customer service and income/cost balance.

income than it would cost. That's more like it. You've thought about who the proposal is for, what they want to hear, and you've given yourself an objective that tells you where you're going and the key elements to focus on en route.

So that's your one-sentence objective. It should have taken you only a few minutes to write, but you're going to be referring to it frequently over the next few hours.

thinking fast

THE RIGHT PROPOSAL

Have you ever presented a proposal only to be told: 'No, no. That's not what I wanted.'? If you've been asked to write a proposal by someone else, it can easily happen. Your boss might say, 'I can't present this to the board. They've agreed the principle of extra staffing already. I want them to agree the logistics – which extra posts to create, who should fill them, who trains them … that sort of thing.'

But there's a simple way to avoid this colossal waste of time: write a clear objective and then show it to your boss (or whoever commissioned the proposal). If you've got it wrong, you've only wasted five minutes rather than hours or even days.

You may not need any longer to set your objective next time. But sometimes it takes a little while to research, so it's worth allowing this time. You might need to find out more about your readers – are they technically minded or not? Are they broadly in agreement or are they likely to take a lot of persuading? What are likely to be the key sticking points in their minds?

You can usually find this out by asking. If you can't ask them directly, ask other people. Colleagues might tell you that the finance director is always a stickler for plenty of financial detail in proposals, or that this particular customer has had after-sales problems in the past and will need convincing that they won't recur if they sign this contract.

So allow yourself time to research your readers – all of them. Not just your bosses, but whoever they will pass your proposal on to. Not just your customer, but the people further up their organization they will show your proposal to. Not just your bank manager, but the regional manager too if you're proposing a sizeable business loan.

Write a clear objective and then show it to your boss

2 collecting
the information

You can't write your report until you know what you want to say. So once you've set your objective, your next task is to collect together all the information you need. And already, your objective is going to come in handy.

The first thing to do is to create a list of areas you need to cover. Begin with the objective, since this covers the most vital aspects of the subject – current problems, staffing levels, customer service, income and costs, for example. You can expand the list with other areas you know you need to touch on as well: speed of service, line of accountability – whatever else applies.

These are broad subject areas of course, so the next step is to create a sub-list under each of these headings. Each of these is a list of specific topics to research. For example, under costs, you might list:

- salaries
- recruitment costs
- induction costs
- overheads

... and so on.

As we'll see in more detail later, you're going to have to come up with hard facts to back up every assertion you make in your proposal. So you're creating a list of all the hard facts you need to research before you begin to write it.

Now write down any other notes of your own of points you want to make, arguments you want to use or benefits you want to emphasize. These are all things you want to include in your proposal which don't necessarily have specific researched facts attached to them. Consider these points for inclusion in your notes:

- **Mention boost to departmental morale – happier staff are more productive.**

- **Accounts always complain paperwork doesn't filter through fast enough – this will help.**

- **Less pressure on staff creates more time to develop projects – customer surveys, improved systems etc.**

The first thing to do is to create a list of areas you need to cover

Write each of these down on a separate piece of paper (for reasons we'll get to in a moment).

Now you have lists covering just about everything that's going to go into this proposal. Don't waste time you haven't got wracking your brain for anything you've missed out – you can always add other points while you're assembling your information. At the moment (just to summarize) you have:

- a list of general areas you need to cover, compiled with reference to your objective

- a list under each of these headings of topics to research and data to collect

- your own notes – each on a separate piece of paper – of other points you want to make that don't require specific data to back them up.

YOU'RE NOT ALONE

If you think you may have missed out something important, you can always ask someone else to run through what they see as the key areas. Call up or e-mail your boss, your customer, a colleague or a member of your team and get them to tell you what they think should be included.

DOING YOUR RESEARCH

The next step is to assemble all the information you've just listed. You can get this information from a variety of sources:

- ▶ **talking to people – suppliers, customers, experts, colleagues**
- ▶ **books**
- ▶ **competitors' annual reports**
- ▶ **minutes of past meetings**
- ▶ **internal management reports and monthly figures**
- ▶ **other internal reports and survey results**
- ▶ **magazine and newspaper articles**
- ▶ **publicly available information and statistics – from trade associations, market research reports, government departments and so on.**

For each topic on your lists, you'll need to decide where you're going to get your information from. You may well have some of it collected already. After all, you may not have started on this proposal until a few minutes ago, but you've probably known it was looming for some time. So you should already have been collecting anything useful – from magazine articles to minutes of meetings – as you have encountered them.

WORKING TO TIME CONSTRAINTS

Ideally, every relevant fact should be in your proposal. But if you simply cannot make enough time to research them all, make sure you research the most important ones. How do you know which those ones are? They are the ones which support your objective.

The question of where to find the information is, generally speaking, easy – there is often only one place where it exists. But if you have a choice, consider which is the most convincing source. Would your readers be more persuaded by a quote from a newspaper article or a statistic from a trade association?

If you cannot track down the data you want, you should question the validity of the argument they were intended to support. Suppose you wanted to say that customers are more concerned about speed of response than about the nature of that response. If you can't back this up, are you sure it's true? And what are you going to say when the board call you in to discuss your interesting proposal and then ask you how you know this?

Some proposals need relatively few hard facts to be convincing, while others need a good deal. If you're under time pressure, you want this proposal to be in the first category. But if you do find yourself trying to research a lot of elusive data in a short time, you might be relieved to know there is a companion volume to this one entitled *Fast Thinking: Finding Facts*, which should be a big help.

ORGANIZING YOUR INFORMATION

No doubt you now have pieces of paper, reports, brochures, books, pamphlets, documents and the like all over your desk. This is the point where you start to sort it all out. The first thing to do is to transfer every piece of information onto its own slip of paper. This is why you wrote down your notes on individual pieces of paper earlier.

Stop panicking: this isn't going to take all day. You don't have to write all the data down – just a note of what is covered and where to find it. So you might have a slip of paper which says 'recruitment costs – *Management Today* article' and a corresponding post-it note in the magazine.

By the end of this process, you will have every single point you want to make in your proposal written down, and you can sort and resort them endlessly (not that you have time to), because each has its own slip of paper. And you should have a neat pile of reference material marked with post-it notes so you can find the data you want really quickly.

FAST FORWARD

If a document or magazine has several pages of useful data marked, number each one on its bookmark and cross-refer to the number on your slip of paper so you can find it fast.

The final part of the process of collecting your information is to sort it into groups. Put all your slips of paper into logical groupings: costs, income, speed, current problems or whatever. This is where having each point written down separately is such an advantage – you can move them around until you feel comfortable with the groupings.

There's no point spending too much time on this, because these groups don't reflect the structure you're going to use for your proposal once you start writing it. But before you start to wonder why on earth, in that case, you have to do it at all, let me explain. There are three particular advantages in doing this.

1 As you work through the pieces of paper, you get the chance to check each one against your objective and make sure you are including only the information you need to. That is not to say that everything will get a specific mention in the objective, obviously, but it will be clear if you're including unnecessary data. You can also check you aren't repeating yourself or including information your readers will already know.

2 As a mental process, the exercise helps to give you a clear focus and to organize your mind.

3 Although these groups do not represent your final structure (which we'll look at in the next chapter), your information will largely stay in these groups as you go along, so you have saved yourself time later.

Since you now have everything down on paper and organized into groups, this is a good point to congratulate yourself on having got this far, and to take a short break. You don't have to retain any information in your head any longer – it's all on your desk now and it's not going anywhere.

The more time you leave yourself, the more convincing the research you can come up with. Sometimes it may make no difference, but often it does.

Suppose one of your key arguments is that some of your competitors have increased the size of their customer service departments, and have seen a corresponding rise in their customer satisfaction ratings. Your readers will want some evidence of this, or at least clear figures on the number of new personnel and the percentage increase in the ratings. Your source for these data might be a colleague who used to work for one of your competitors, and who therefore knows all the relevant facts and figures ... but is on holiday until next week. Whoops. And the proposal has to be finished tomorrow.

That's a big part of why it's always better to start work on a proposal early. This time you might get away with repeating the data from memory and catching up with your colleague as soon as they get back from their holiday. But for next time, it will help to set aside even just a couple of hours a week or two in advance to get the ball rolling on this sort of data which can take a while to track down.

The more time you leave yourself, the more convincing the research you can come up with

3 structure

You're well on your way. You've collected all your information now, and you know exactly what you're going to say. The only question left is: what order will you say it in? This should be easy, but it doesn't always seem to be. You've probably read confused proposals yourself which left you barely more enlightened at the end than you were at the beginning. I remember wading through a pretty hefty proposal once only to find myself still asking at the end, 'Yes, but what are you actually selling?'

A lot of the trouble stems from the fact that it is so abundantly clear to *you* what you are trying to say that it can be difficult to see the issue from your readers' perspective. Maybe they know nothing about your product at all. Maybe what seems to you like a blindingly obvious idea somehow does nothing for them. So you have to keep reminding yourself of the differences between you and them. For example:

- **They don't know what your product, service or idea can do.**
- **They have different priorities from you.**
- **They don't know the background which brought you to this point.**
- **They don't know what the alternatives are.**
- **They don't see why things can't just carry on as they are.**

A proposal that doesn't address these differences – doesn't take the reader along the logical route through your argument – is never going to be a persuasive and influential document. Even if all the information they need *is* in there somewhere, it must be coherently presented and argued if it is to leave them clearer on the subject, let alone persuaded of your case.

thinking smart

DEVIL'S ADVOCATE

It can help to put yourself in your readers' shoes for a minute. Suppose they are really resistant to your idea. Imagine what they would pick holes in: 'What's the point of that?' 'What's wrong with the way we do things already?' and so on. You can even get a colleague to play the role of Negative Reader In A Bad Mood for you. It should help you see that what is obvious to you isn't obvious to them.

The good news is that there is a way of presenting the information in your proposal that is clear, logical and persuasive, and that works every time. Whether you are proposing a major sale to a client, an idea for a product to a manufacturer, or a new system to your board of directors, this structure is always the best way to do it.

Just as a good story should always have a beginning, a middle and an end, so a good proposal should always follow the same structure. There are lots of different ways of expressing it: setting the scene, developing the story, resolving the story; or maybe situation, complication, resolution. Whatever terminology you use, they all mean the same thing. One of the easiest to remember is:

- **position**
- **problem**
- **proposal.**

To begin with, you need to state the current position. Then you look at the problem – why the situation has to change. Then you make your proposal in the light of this background. Actually, there is often more than one possible solution, although you will have your own preferred one. If this is the case you will need to discuss the others too, so you can insert another section. Just for the sake of mnemonics (the four Ps), we'll call it possibilities. So now your structure looks like this:

- position
- problem
- possibilities
- proposal.

One reason this structure is so easy to follow is because we have all grown up listening to stories that follow this format – and reading books and watching movies that run along the same lines. To go back to basics, let's take Hansel and Gretel as an example:

1 **Position.** Hansel and Gretel were left in the woods by their parents who couldn't afford to look after them any longer.

2 **Problem.** They found a house made of gingerbread, but, unfortunately, it belonged to a wicked witch who imprisoned them.

3 **Possibilities.** They could try to escape or they could trick the witch. Otherwise they would be cooked and eaten by her.

4 **Proposal.** In the end the best option was to trick the witch by pushing her into her own oven so she burned to death, and then to run away. So Hansel and Gretel escaped and ran home.

A good proposal should have a beginning, a middle and an end

See? All you're doing when you write a proposal is spinning a good yarn (and hopefully one which is a little more suitable for children). You don't have to follow an alien format – just the structure you've grown up understanding naturally. Boy meets girl, boy loses girl, boy finds girl. Manager wants something, boss says no, manager persuades boss.

ARE YOU SITTING COMFORTABLY?

It can be easier to get a handle on the structure by telling yourself the contents of the proposal as a story. Begin with: 'Once upon a time there was a manager …' (or a business, or whatever). You should find it quite easy to slip into storytelling mode (especially if you have children), and you should find much of your proposal structure slots into place.

And there's more good news. Yes, really. It is much quicker writing to a clear structure than floundering around trying to decide what to say next. The structure makes most of your decisions for you. So you can just get on with getting the proposal down on paper. Let's now look at each element of the structure in turn.

POSITION

Start your proposal by stating the current position. You might consider this to be stating the obvious, but do it anyway. For one thing, it may not be as obvious as you think. You may want extra staff in your department because you are struggling to maintain customer service standards, but some of your readers may not realize you're struggling. If you never explain this, they'll read the whole proposal on the assumption that you are asking for the luxury of extra staff rather than the necessity.

Or suppose you're proposing to a retail outlet that they stock your new range of citrus juicers. You might start by stating that juicers always sell well, especially in the summer. Tell them how many a typical outlet sells each week. Otherwise they might

PAPER CHASE

At this stage you can jot down what you want to say in draft form (we'll be looking at phrasing and language and all that later) as you go along. However, it can be quicker – and just as helpful – simply to organize your slips of paper as you go. Begin by creating a small pile of things to state in the 'position' part of your proposal and build the slips of paper up from there.

be working on the assumption that your juicers are terrific, but no one wants juicers these days.

So you need to make sure that all your readers are starting in the same position. But there are other reasons too for summarizing your position at the start of the proposal.

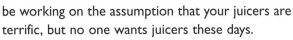 It helps people to focus on the right part of the issue. If you've written a proposal for your board of directors, some of the non-executive members might know that your proposal is something to do with needing more company cars, say, but may not have realized that it was specifically about the need for the PR department to have cars.

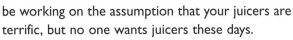 It shows that you understand the background. The readers are far more likely to accept your proposed solution if they can see that you understand the problem.

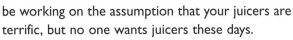 It gives you a chance to explain things to anyone who doesn't understand the problem without patronizing anyone who does. The tone isn't 'I'm telling you this because you don't know it'; it's 'Let's just make sure we're all agreed exactly what we're talking about.'

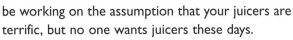 Your intended reader might decide to pass your proposal on to someone else much less acquainted with the subject. Your customer might be fully conversant in the state of the market for citrus juicers, but what if they pass your proposal on to their regional director who doesn't know a juicer from a squeezer?

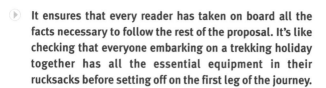

It ensures that every reader has taken on board all the facts necessary to follow the rest of the proposal. It's like checking that everyone embarking on a trekking holiday together has all the essential equipment in their rucksacks before setting off on the first leg of the journey.

You may find that you can state the position in a single sentence, or it may take a while to explain – you identified your readers' level of knowledge when you worked out your objective. Obviously if it's relatively low you may need to explain quite a lot. You may also have to run through a bit of history to explain how the present position was reached – that's fine, if it helps the reader.

Stating the position also gives you a chance to prove that you understand things from the reader's point of view. This is especially valuable if you're writing a sales proposal. Suppose your company sells photocopiers. Your proposal to a potential customer should not start by telling them *your* position – that your company 'started out selling printing blocks back in 1657 and now markets a range of photocopiers'. The idea is to state the *reader's* position. So you start by saying that they 'have a photocopier which they've leased for the last 12 years' and so on. Of course your position might be the same as the reader's; or it might not – it's not important. *Their* position is the one that matters.

From the start of your proposal onwards – in other words from here – you must deal in facts, not assumptions or unsupported assertions. It is facts that will persuade your readers, and facts alone. No matter how much of a rush you are in to get this proposal written, facts are not the place to economize.

So don't just say that the market in citrus juicers is very healthy – say precisely how healthy it is. State the rate of growth or the level of sales (and before you ask, no, it's not OK to make it up).

LYING WITH STATISTICS

You might think you can remember a particular statistic even though you can't quite track it down just at the moment, so you might as well include it. Or if you're a good bullshitter, you may even be tempted to embellish facts. *Don't do it*. What if someone asks you for evidence, or tries to check your sources? Sooner or later it will happen – if not this proposal, the next one or the one after. It would cast doubt on all the other facts you ever present, including the real ones. Just imagine what it could do to your reputation and your career ... and resist temptation.

PROBLEM

The point of this section of the proposal is to establish why you need to do anything at all – why the present position can't continue. This could be something bad, but it doesn't have to be. It could be an opportunity that you mustn't miss. Look at these examples.

Bad

▷ **Demand is changing.**

▷ **Equipment is wearing out.**

▷ **Staff are leaving.**

▷ **Money is being wasted.**

▷ **There is new competition in the market.**

▷ **Offices are becoming overcrowded.**

Good

▷ **There is scope for a new product.**

▷ **A small investment in new equipment could increase profit margins.**

▷ **There's a new source of raw materials which is much cheaper than before.**

▷ **A perfect site has come up on the new trading estate.**

▷ **Trade barriers to Europe are coming down.**

▷ **New legislation means things are possible that weren't before.**

This is the section of the proposal most likely to meet with resistance from the reader, so it's especially important to validate your statement of the problem with hard evidence. The idea is that by the time you've finished explaining the problem, the reader should be left in no doubt that Something Must Be Done. All that remains is to bring them round to your view of precisely *what* should be done.

POSSIBILITIES

You may or may not want to consider different options for resolving the problem that your reader is now convinced exists. Or rather, the reader may or may not want to consider them – that's the factor that should determine whether or not you include a 'possibilities' section in your proposal. Your reader is likely to be adopting one of two stances:

1 They will decide whether to do x, y or z.

2 They will either accept your proposal or leave things as they are.

In the first of these situations, they will consider other options whether you do or not. If you own a car wash, say, any potential customer will consider the options of using your car wash, washing their car themselves, getting the kid round the corner to

It's always worth making sure you've considered all the options that may have occurred to your readers. If you discuss two other options but miss out their favourite one, you have missed an opportunity to compare yours favourably with it. So think it through for a moment. The most commonly missed option is … doing nothing at all. For example, you may have considered your two leading competitors, but forgotten that your customer might simply leave things as they are and stock no citrus juicers at all.

However, if your reader is simply going to say yes or no, there's no need to consider alternatives. If you're asking your bank manager for a loan for a new business you're starting, they won't be choosing between yours and someone else's – they'll give you both a loan if you both warrant one. It's a straight yes or no choice; you can't very well include a section on their other options when there aren't any.

do it for 50p, or leaving it dirty. You may only be offering one of the four options, but you'll need to discuss the other three with your customers in order to convince them that your option is better.

So if you're writing a proposal for a customer who is likely to be considering other options, you'll need to include a 'possibilities' section in order to discuss

Your readers will consider other options whether you do or not.

them. Or if the board is considering your proposal for restructuring, but also considering a more minor restructure, or the option of leaving things alone – you'll need to cover these in your report.

This section should cover the pros and cons of each possibility, such as:

- how each one works or what it does (just in case the readers do not already know)
- what it costs
- other relevant details such as how long it takes to implement, technical specifications etc.
- what its benefits are (it's the cheapest, it's very safe, customers seem to love it, it only takes two people to operate it)
- what its disadvantages are (delivery takes four months, the staff hate using it, there's no absolute guarantee it will work etc.).

You may want to look at these factors for each option in isolation, but you will probably want to compare them as well. Don't draw any overall conclusions at this stage – that comes later. You may have your own preferred possibility but it shouldn't be visible to the reader at this stage. You must describe all the possibilities fairly and impartially.

THE POSSIBILITIES ARE ENDLESS ...

You'll just confuse your readers if you include 25 possibilities at this stage. The ideal number is about three (including yours). But it could be two or it could be four. Maybe even five. Any more, and you're better off grouping them together – instead of listing all the options for restructuring in your proposal for extra staffing, simply include 'restructuring' as an alternative to extra staffing.

Preserve neutrality

I know it can go against the grain to give a fair hearing to a hated rival contender, but it has to be done. The thing is, one of your readers might have a secret – or indeed an overt – preference for another option. If you pooh-pooh it, they will resent you and won't be inclined to listen to your own preference. But if you demonstrate that their view is valid, they are more likely to give you a fair hearing in return.

You must describe all the possibilities fairly and impartially

The psychology of persuasion is worth considering. The process of reading a proposal is more emotional (albeit unconsciously) than you might think. The reader needs to feel that you understand their position. In a sense, it shows that you accept them, it puts you both on the same team. This feeling of acceptance is surprisingly important, even to the most hard-bitten business people. In other words, you have to start by convincing them that you're on their side.

Once you're standing alongside your readers – they've accepted you and they're confident that you've accepted them – you can gently start to lead them where you want them to go. You can explain things from their perspective and guide them towards the right decision. They're much more likely to listen to you when you're standing next to them. If you were miles away shouting, 'Come over here – it's much nicer, honest!' they could reasonably ask, 'How do you know? You don't know what it's like over here.'

So that's the key to the psychology. Don't stand in your entrenched position shouting, 'Come here!' If you want them to agree to the idea you're proposing, *you* have to do the work. Go over to them, take their hand and lead them back to your position. You can show you're on their side by being fair and objective, and not dismissing the other possibilities.

PROPOSAL

If you're not including a 'possibilities' section this will probably be the largest part of the document. It will include:

- **an explanation of what you are proposing (your business plan, for example, for your bank manager)**

- **answers to any objections which you anticipate from your readers (such as the bank manager saying, 'But why do you need as much as £25,000?')**

- **facts and figures to support your case (such as research showing there is a market gap for your proposed product).**

ththththi **thinking smart**

GIVE THEM AN EXCUSE

Some of your readers may already have expressed strong views on the subject your proposal is about. And people don't like backing down. So give them an excuse to change their minds. Enable them to say: 'You see, I was right. It will mean a lot of overtime. Mind you, if there are long-term benefits we didn't know about ...'

If you have listed the 'possibilities', you will already have covered these points. In this case, the 'proposal' section should read a bit like the television show *Call My Bluff*: 'I don't think it's the first one; it sounded rather implausible. A sort of medieval alarm clock? I think not ...' – that sort of thing. Except that you don't want to be rude about any of the options – if your readers support the other option, or if they did until they just read this stonking proposal persuading them otherwise, you are criticizing their judgement if you throw scorn on it.

You've already discussed the pros and cons of each option under 'possibilities', so now you simply make a choice and justify it: 'All in all the brick house looks like the best option. The straw one will blow over too easily and the wood one, while it is slightly more stable, is nevertheless also vulnerable to fire. The brick one, on the other hand, should withstand any amount of wind and it won't burn. It's true that it's the most expensive, but its durability means that in the long term, say ten years, it's actually the cheapest of the three options. What's more, it's the only one that's truly secure against wolves, as the survey figures show.'

The biggest danger when you prepare your proposal in something of a hurry is that you will miss out some key fact or argument, or even overlook one of the other options. If you have more time it is a good idea to draft out your proposal, however roughly, at this stage and ask someone else to cast their eye over it – your boss or a close colleague who knows the background is ideal. This should not only bring to light any important missing pieces, but will also reassure you that you have everything covered.

Apart from that, one of the great things about working to a clear and logical structure is that it is actually the quickest way of doing something. So even though you're fretting about the time, you have the satisfaction of knowing that more time wouldn't have helped you do the job any better – you've already done it perfectly.

Make a choice and justify it

4 good
writing style

This is the scary bit for a lot of people – choosing the right words and phrases to sound articulate and intelligent, and to get the argument across strong and clear. Let's be honest, you're worried that the reader will stop thinking about the proposal itself, and start wondering where you were educated (if at all) and how on earth your career has made it this far.

If it's any help, this is most people's worry when they write a proposal, and yet they actually do fine. And so will you. However, we don't want to settle for 'fine'. So this chapter is partly about reassuring you of the right way to do things, and partly about making sure that your style really shines. The next chapter, by the way, is about using correct English – grammar and all that stuff – so we're not going to worry about that just now. For the moment, here's a crash course in becoming a skilled, articulate and persuasive writer.

CREATING AN IMPRESSION

Many people try too hard to impress when they write. They use long, convoluted sentences packed with long, convoluted words. But, in fact, this doesn't impress at all – it does quite the opposite. Your readers aren't marking an essay, they are trying to decide whether to buy into your idea or your product. They want the reading bit to be easy and straightforward, so they can concentrate on the content, not the style.

And that is the crux of it. Everything about using a good writing style is to do with making your proposal simple and easy to read. You're not James Joyce – the MD isn't going to take your proposal on holiday for a spot of thought-provoking and inspirational literature to read on the beach. Your readers want the message to come through clear and simple. They won't be impressed by 'clever' writing. If you keep all your words and sentences short and simple, they will be deeply grateful. Anyway, for all you know, they may not understand half those long words other people use, and making your readers feel uneducated and inadequate isn't going to endear you to them.

WRITE AS YOU SPEAK

As a rule of thumb, if you don't use a word in everyday speech, don't use it in your proposal. If you wouldn't say, 'Let me draw your attention to the aforementioned point …' don't write it. Just write, 'As I mentioned before …'

So the first rule of good writing is keep it simple:

- **short paragraphs**
- **short sentences**
- **short words.**

This is all pretty easy so far, isn't it? And that's how it stays. A good writing style is much quicker to write, because you don't have to agonize over constructing complex phrases or remembering little-used words.

Certain types of words are particular culprits when it comes to making proposals harder on the reader:

- **legal words (heretofore, notwithstanding and all that lot).**
- **pomposity (henceforth, thus and so on).**
- **jargon.**

Regarding this last point: *Never* try to impress with jargon. The only time you should use it is when there is absolutely no other word that will do. And then – unless your readers are all without doubt fully conversant in the jargon – add an explanation in brackets. If you have to use several jargon words you can add a glossary at the end.

STYLE THAT SELLS

All we're doing at the moment is knocking out all the complicated bits to keep your writing simple. But there are other types of word or phrase that are also best avoided. Look, if you're in a real hurry, I know it's tempting to skip this bit. But try to resist, because it's about how to make your proposal more convincing, and that's the most important thing here. You need to sell your idea to

thinking smart

CHAT BUT NOT SLANG

Use idiomatic English when it comes to your vocabulary, although slang is pushing it a bit far. So you can talk about the lavatory (assuming it's relevant to your proposal), you don't have to call it the toilet or the washroom. Just don't call it the bog.

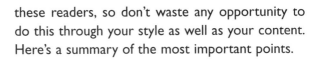

these readers, so don't waste any opportunity to do this through your style as well as your content. Here's a summary of the most important points.

Use concrete nouns. Ouch! Noun? That was definitely one of those words your English teacher used to use. In fact, it could even be defined as jargon, couldn't it? OK, I'll explain it in case you weren't concentrating hard enough at school (as if). Nouns are words for things: car, dog, holiday, phone, newspaper. And the ones I just listed are all concrete nouns – they give the reader a clear visual picture of something specific. They're fine.

The ones to avoid are the abstract ones, especially the ones that give no clear picture. For example: situation, activities, operation. Reading them just bores people. And it makes it harder for them to grasp what you are saying. You can't always avoid abstract nouns, but you often can. For example, instead of saying 'When you take into *consideration* …', say 'When you consider …'. Here's another example: Change 'the *operation* of this bulldozer isn't easy' to 'this bulldozer isn't easy to operate.'

Use active verbs. Done it again! More jargon! OK, a verb is a doing word: run, help, find, operate, over-exaggerate … and so on. Active verbs are ones where the subject of the sentence is doing something – 'I *met* an important customer yesterday.' The baddies are the passive verbs, where things happen to the subject: 'I *was met* by an important customer yesterday.' Again, these are slow and plodding, while plenty of active verbs give your proposal a lively, dynamic feel, full of action.

Here are a couple more examples. Instead of saying 'I *was trampled* by the elephant,' say: 'The elephant *trampled* me.' Instead of writing 'The aeroplane *will be painted* by a team of people wearing magnetic boots,' say: 'A team of people wearing magnetic boots *will paint* the aeroplane.'

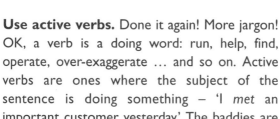

GETTING IT THE RIGHT WAY ROUND

If you want to be sure you are using an active verb, just ask yourself what is doing the action in the sentence – and then put that first. If you were trampled by an elephant, the elephant is doing the trampling. So put the elephant first in the sentence, and it all follows naturally: The elephant trampled me.

Avoid clichés. Overused phrases cease to mean anything because the reader's eye just skims over them. So you're wasting an opportunity if you use empty phrases such as *meeting customer needs* or *a wide range of products and services*. Almost invariably there's a better way of saying the same thing. Instead of 'a wide range of products and services', why not say what they are? Or at least give an idea: 'Over 30 different vehicles, from two-door sports cars to four-ton trucks'. It's much clearer, and gives the reader a concrete visual image (you're also changing abstract nouns – 'products' and 'services' – into concrete ones).

Avoid stock phrases. How often do you hear people say 'at this precise moment in time' when what they mean is 'now'? Business English seems to be full of this kind of cumbersome and slightly pompous phrase. The problem with using these

YOU AND I

In the interests of a clear style, in which you write as you speak, address your reader as 'you' and refer to yourself as 'I'. It's fine to say, 'You'll be able to see the improvement within a few weeks' or 'I'd like to explain how it works…'.

phrases is that they give your reader time to lose the thread of the sentence, make you sound like everyone else, and give the whole document a slightly woolly feel. In other words, they do nothing for your image as an original thinker and a dynamic manager.

Here are a few more to avoid: there is a reasonable expectation that … (probably); owing to the situation that … (because); should a situation arise where … (if); taking into consideration such factors as … (considering); prior to the occasion when … (before). There. You should have the idea by now.

Avoid neutral words. Neutral words are inexpressive ones such as 'alter', 'affect', or 'express an opinion'. Your style will be much more colourful and interesting if you replace these with more expressive alternatives. So instead of writing 'the new flexitime system altered productivity' write that it 'improved' or 'boosted' it.

IT'S…

Unless your readers are very fusty and old fashioned, it's fine to elide words. In other words you can write 'it's' instead of 'it is', 'isn't' instead of 'is not', and 'can't' instead of 'cannot'.

BROAD STYLE

So much for the individual words and phrases you use. But how about your broader style? We've already talked about using everyday language, which means addressing the reader as 'you' and yourself as 'I'. But there are a few other points worth making about your overall style.

Match the style to the reader

This is a general approach, not something to get hung up on. You don't have to write in the same style as your reader would. But be sensitive to them. If you are writing for most readers, the guidelines so far in this chapter will do you fine. Just skim through this section to make sure you don't need to read it. But some types of readers do need a slight tweak of style to keep them happy.

Adapting your style to suit your reader is one of the best subliminal techniques for showing you're on their side – it makes them feel that you're their sort of person. So if your readers are much older or younger than you, for example, adapt your style a little accordingly:

Old fashioned readers. If your readers were at school 40 years ago, they may be fussier than you about 'correct' grammar (that is to say, grammar that was correct forty years ago). So you're probably better off using words like 'whom'. And sticking to 'proper' sentences. If you've never met your readers but you suspect they're old fashioned – perhaps they're a group of elderly barristers, for instance – steer away from the most obvious modern colloquialisms. And don't start sentences with 'and'.

Young readers. Conversely, if you use words like 'whom' when you're writing for most young readers, you'll alienate them. Don't break the rules (outlined in the next chapter) completely, but feel free to stretch them. The readers will feel you're on their wavelength.

Readers with restricted reading skills. Perhaps some of your readers are foreign and their English is poor. Or maybe the report is for your boss who is mildly dyslexic. If, for any reason, your readers might have problems with standard English, or with certain words, adapt your style to avoid their problem areas. If your readers don't speak good English, the ideal solution is to have the proposal or report translated. Failing that, however, it would be better to replace the word 'livelihood' with 'job', for instance, or 'archive' with 'records'.

SAY IT OUT LOUD

If you're not sure whether something goes in terms of your readers' own style, play safe. If you can't think of a safe option that says what you want to so succinctly, imagine standing in the room with your readers giving a presentation (which is, after all, only a spoken proposal rather than a written one). If you would use the word or phrase in a presentation, you can use it in a proposal. If not, not.

Be politically correct

This topic gets almost everybody incredibly heated – whatever their view. But it doesn't matter what *your* view is of course; it's the reader's view that counts. If you're in any doubt at all, don't take chances. The fact is that this particular subject is now so well discussed that anyone who doesn't follow the modern approach appears, at best, to be fuddy-duddy and out of touch. So make sure your reports and proposals are free of racism, ageism, sexism and any other -isms you can think of, regardless of your personal views.

Avoiding sexism is the area that can cause most problems. All the other subjects or words that are not 'pc' are pretty easy to avoid. But it can seem quite difficult to avoid any reference to gender except when talking about real people. So here are a few tips:

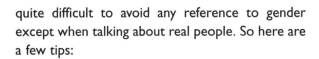 **Rewrite the sentence in the plural:** instead of 'England believes that every man will do his duty' write 'England believes that all citizens will do their duty.'

- It's now generally acceptable to use the pronoun 'they' in place of 'he' or 'she', so instead of 'Ask your boss if he or she wants a cup of tea' you can say 'Ask your boss if they want a cup of tea.' Occasionally, this construction can sound uncomfortable, however, in which case use one of the alternative techniques to avoid referring to gender altogether.

- You can use the phrase 'he or she' (or variations on it such as s/he). This can be intrusive, however, and tends to draw attention to itself. It's certainly correct, but it may not always be the smoothest approach.

- Say 'you' or 'your'. For example, instead of saying 'Every employee should leave his desk tidy' say 'Leave your desk tidy.' Apart from being more correct, this is also a much friendlier style to adopt.

Explain new ideas clearly

You must know the old challenge: explain a spiral staircase without using your hands. Well, with reports and proposals you can never use your hands. Sometimes you can provide diagrams and drawings, but not if you're explaining an abstract concept. What's more, you won't be there when your readers see the document, so they can't stop you as they could at a presentation and ask you to run that one past them again.

One solution that frequently works is to use examples. A clear example or two can make all the difference between clarity and bafflement. For instance (you see, I'm giving you an example): I mentioned earlier that you should use concrete nouns. Now, if you didn't know what a noun was, you'd have been baffled. But as soon as I gave you some examples – car, dog, holiday, phone, newspaper – it should have become perfectly clear.

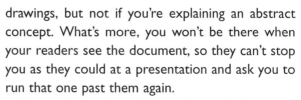

thinking smart

IF IN DOUBT ...

It's difficult to give too many examples. Something may be evident to you, but not necessarily so obvious to your readers. If you think there's any chance that the reader might benefit from an example, supply one or even several. No one's going to complain if you give them an example they didn't really need.

Use metaphors and analogies

These are also invaluable devices, especially for explaining abstract concepts and ideas. For instance (here we go again; I'm giving you another example!), I said earlier that the way to persuade someone round to your way of thinking was to 'show that you're on their side' and then 'lead them over to your side'. When you are trying to explain an abstract concept, the best way is often to find a concrete visual image to relate it to.

Analogies tend to start 'it's a bit like ...' or 'it's as if ...'. Suppose you're trying to explain how white blood cells work. You could say, 'They're a bit like a school of piranha, swimming gently along. As soon as anything alien appears in their river, they descend on it and attack it mercilessly until they've eaten it. Then they go back to drifting in the current again.'

The key thing with examples, metaphors and analogies is knowing when to use them. If you're writing about a new drug for treating heart disease, and your readership is a group of senior consultants who specialize in cardiac disorders, there's no point explaining where in the body the heart is located. But if you're writing for heart patients, they'll need things explained that the consultants would take for granted.

NO NEED TO EXPLAIN?

If you're in any doubt about whether your proposal is as clear as it should be, ask a plain-speaking and honest colleague or friend to read your first draft and tell you if you need to explain anything more clearly. Obviously you need to ask someone whose knowledge of the subject is not substantially different from that of the readers.

START WRITING

That's the end of the crash course in clear and persuasive writing. So now you can sit down and write your proposal, following these guidelines to make sure it is not only well structured but well written too. You can use the next chapter to help correct any technical points of grammar and so on after you've finished your draft. After that there's a little more to do, but you've done the bulk of the work.

Here's a checklist to help you keep your writing on course as you go.

Checklist

Keep it simple
- ▶ **short paragraphs**
- ▶ **short sentences**
- ▶ **short words.**

Use a style that sells
- ▶ **use concrete nouns**
- ▶ **use active verbs**
- ▶ **avoid clichés**
- ▶ **avoid stock phrases**
- ▶ **avoid neutral words**
- ▶ **beware ambiguous words.**

Broad style
- ▶ **match the style to the reader**
- ▶ **be politically correct**
- ▶ **explain new ideas with examples, metaphors and analogies.**

As with the structure of your proposal, this is both the best style to use and as quick as any other – certainly as quick as any other effective style. But you will find that when you have more time, you'll almost certainly feel more comfortable taking a couple of drafts to get to this stage. You might find it easier to write the proposal in a simple style first, then go through it looking for places where you could usefully add examples or analogies, and then go through it again checking for jargon, clichés and neutral words and all the other things on the checklist.

After this you can redraft the whole thing with all the changes, and then give it one final read through. And the last stage you should always incorporate if you can possibly find the time is to get someone else whose opinion you value to read it through for you.

Have a break — we're nearly there.

If you can find the time, get someone else to read it through for you

5 using correct English

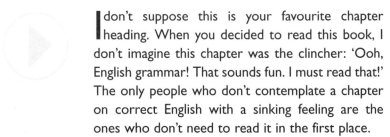

I don't suppose this is your favourite chapter heading. When you decided to read this book, I don't imagine this chapter was the clincher: 'Ooh, English grammar! That sounds fun. I must read that!' The only people who don't contemplate a chapter on correct English with a sinking feeling are the ones who don't need to read it in the first place.

So if no one's interested in this chapter, what is it doing in the book? Why don't we just gloss over this bit? Can't a spelling and grammar check do it all for you anyway?

We'll get to spell checks in a minute. But first, why are you supposed to read this stuff? If it didn't sink in at school, it's hardly likely to now, is it? Well, at school, nothing was riding on it. But now you have an incentive: your proposal – even your success – could depend on it. The trouble is simple: What if your readers can spell? And punctuate, and remember when to put the apostrophe in 'its' and all the rest of it? In other words, what if they notice when you get it wrong?

The answer is that they will be distinctly unimpressed. They may disregard a stray typing error, but their opinion of you will be diminished if they perceive you as someone who can't use English properly. Even if the proposal is otherwise excellent and they accept it, they will still be left with a feeling that you're not quite up to their standard. And if your bosses are reading the proposal, that might even affect your career.

You may yearn for the days of Olde Englande when there was no right and wrong in spelling and grammar. And you may argue convincingly that it's stupid to put a 'c' in practice some of the time and an 's' the rest of the time. But your protestations are wasted on the kind of directors and customers who know the difference between a compliment and a complement.

So this chapter stays in.

SPELL CHECKS AND GRAMMAR CHECKS

We'll begin by addressing this question. If you are in a tearing rush, you can use these. In fact, you can use them anyway if you like. *But they are not infallible.* Mistakes can still slip through. They are better than nothing, but they can give you a false sense of security.

The problem with spell checks is simple: If you mistype or misspell a word in a way which happens to be another word rather than gobbledegook, your spell check won't pick it up. If you miss the final 'o' off 'too' you are left with a legitimate word ('to'). Your spell check has no quarrel with this word, so it will leave it alone … even though it is grammatically wrong.

Grammar checks are quite often plain wrong. They have no common sense, and they often misinterpret what you have typed and try to change it when there's nothing wrong with it. If you are fairly confident on your grammar you might find them helpful for picking up errors so long as you know when to hit the 'ignore' button. But if you're very shaky they are likely to give you a bum steer as often as not. What's more, they can take ages, and you're in a hurry.

thinking smart

FINAL CHECK

The best way to use a spell check or a grammar check is as a final run through, *after* you have checked the proposal by eye. That prevents you relying on them too heavily.

So, while computer checks are useful as a safety net, they won't do everything for you. They'll correct you if you spell embarrass with only one 'r', but they won't tell you if you inadvertently spell principle with an '-al' at the end.

So the answer, I'm afraid, is to know for yourself when you are right and when you are wrong, just in case your readers can tell too. So let's have a really quick check through some of the main sticking points. If you're in a rush don't read this right through for the moment, just use the chapter as a reference for the bits you need.

If you do stick with it, you'll be rewarded at the end with a list of rules you are allowed to break. I bet your English teacher never gave you that.

VOCABULARY

If you're shaky, don't use words you're not sure of. That's the general rule. But sometimes you have to. So use a dictionary and look up anything you're not 100 per cent confident on. In addition to that, there are certain frequently misused words which it is worth making sure you know about. One of the most obvious examples is 'criteria'. This is a plural word, so if there is only one of them, you should say 'criterion'. Once you've learnt that, you're already in an elite group.

Here is a list of ten pairs of the most commonly confused words and their meanings – see how many of these pairs you already know.

affect verb meaning to influence: It affected me deeply	**effect** noun meaning result, or verb meaning to bring about: It had a deep effect on me / The new law will effect change in the country
adverse adjective meaning unfavourable: It had an adverse effect on me	**averse** adjective meaning opposed to or disinclined: I am averse to powdered eggs (formerly 'averse from')
principle noun meaning a standard or rule of conduct: It's against my principles to do that	**principal** adjective or noun meaning most important: the principal rule, the principal of the school
stationery noun meaning writing materials: I'm running out of stationery	**stationary** adjective meaning not moving: That is a stationary vehicle
complement noun meaning something that completes, or verb meaning to make complete: One more member of the committee would give us a full complement	**compliment** noun meaning praise or verb meaning to praise: She complimented me on paying her such a kind compliment

council noun meaning an assembly of people: The council meets every month	**counsel** verb meaning to recommend, or noun meaning recommendation: I counselled her to accept my counsel
dependent adjective meaning reliant: I'm dependent on my job for my income	**dependant** – noun meaning a person who depends: He has three elderly dependants
ensure verb meaning to make certain: I want to ensure that the water's not too hot before I get in the bath	**insure** verb meaning to protect against risk: I have insured my car against being damaged by circus animals
practice noun: I need more practice before I can do this	**practise** verb: I'm going to practise the double bass until I'm an expert
advice noun meaning recommendation: Let me give you some advice	**advise** verb meaning to counsel: I advise you to think twice before you do that

SPELLING

Use a dictionary, and a spell check for a final sweep of your proposal, but in the meantime here are some basic guidelines for spelling:

- Why does targeted have one 't' in the middle and regretted have two? There's a rule you can follow here: If the stress falls on the final syllable of the word (regret), you double the final letter when you add -ed. If it falls on an earlier syllable (target) you retain the single letter at the end. Other examples of retaining the single letter include marketed, offered, focused, benefited. A final 'l', however is always doubled, as in travelled.

- If you are turning an adjective ending in a single or double 'l' (magical, full, special, dull) into an adverb, you always end up with a double 'll' in the middle: magically, fully, specially, dully.

- The rule 'i before e except after c' is worth remembering. The exceptions are, or can be:
  - words in which the 'ei' is *not* pronounced 'ee' (such as heinous or inveigle)
  - the word seize
  - some names of places and people.

*ththithi*thinking smart

PATRIOTIC STYLE

The Americans tend to end words -ize which we end -ise (organise, rationalise, subsidise). If you think your readers would prefer the English form, use the -ise ending.

ABBREVIATIONS

However fast you're trying to get this proposal written, there's no point saving time by using abbreviations such as approx for approximately (I hope you're not *that* desperate). It implies the reader isn't important enough to bother writing it out fully for.

However, it is always worth shortening long titles to their initials, such as EC for European Community. It saves your reader having to wade through the whole thing each time. The first time you mention the organization, use its full name. If you're going to refer to it later, add its abbreviation in brackets afterwards – for example, local education authority (LEA). After that, you can use the initials on their own.

APOSTROPHES

The apostrophe is probably the most frequently misused piece of punctuation in the English language. People most commonly misuse it when they want to pluralize a word, for example:

Wrong

▶ **Pick your own tomatoe's**

▶ **Back in the 1880's ...**

▶ **All the department's were represented.**

All these examples are wrong, for a very good reason – you don't need an apostrophe *anywhere* to pluralize a word. That isn't what apostrophes were invented for. They actually have two purposes:

1 to show possession
2 to show that a letter has been missed out.

The possessive

Add an 's to the person, people or thing doing the possessing: the children's shoes, the tree's shade, the snake's eyes. The apostrophe goes after whoever is possessing, so in the last example, if you were talking about the eyes of lots of snakes the apostrophe would go after the final 's' of snakes: the snakes' eyes.

thinkingsfast

PLACING THE APOSTROPHE

A quick way to remember where the apostrophe goes is to say to yourself 'the ... belonging to the ... ':

- If they're the *eyes* belonging to the *snake* (singular) you would write: the snake's eyes.

- If they're the *eyes* belonging to the *snakes* (plural) you would write: the snakes' eyes.

If the person or people (or snakes) doing the possessing already have an 's' on the end, you don't add another one; simply stick the apostrophe on the end – that's why you've never seen anyone write 'the snakes's eyes'. The only times when you would add an 's' after a singular word that ends in 's' are:

- if it's a proper name (Mr Jones's, St James's)
- if the word ends in a double 'ss' (the boss's).

Never use an apostrophe with a possessive pronoun. Oops! Jargon again. (It's a fair cop. A possessive pronoun is a word indicating possession which replaces someone or something's name.) These are words like yours, hers, its, theirs, ours.

Missing letters

You also use an apostrophe to show that one or more letters have been left out, as in: isn't, shouldn't (both missing the 'o' of 'not'), what's (meaning 'what is' or 'what has'), can't (for cannot) and so on.

Perhaps one of the most frequent confusions is between *its* and *it's*: they are two completely different words. *Its* is a possessive pronoun (you know what that is now) and therefore has no apostrophe, while *it's* is short for *it is* and does have one. The easiest way to tell each time you write the word is to say it in your head as 'it is'. If it makes sense, it's short for it is and has an apostrophe. Otherwise it doesn't. For example:

1 'I gave the dog its breakfast.'
2 Try the technique: 'I gave the dog it is breakfast.'
3 That was gobbledegook. It clearly isn't short for it is, so it doesn't have an apostrophe.

Here's another example:

1 'Its a great day to go potholing.'
2 Try the technique: 'It is a great day to go potholing.'
3 That makes sense – it's short for 'it is' so it *does* have an apostrophe, in place of the missing 'i'.

RULES YOU CAN BREAK

OK, I promised. So here it is. Three traditional rules of English grammar which haven't made it into the 21st century. If you're writing for well-educated octogenarians you might think twice about breaking them, but no one else cares two hoots any more.

Never start a sentence with 'and', 'but' or 'because'
William Blake clearly wasn't too bothered by grammatic convention when he wrote

And did those feet, in ancient times.

And not only can you start a sentence with these words, you can start paragraphs with them too. They can be very useful for this purpose, as they tend to add emphasis to what you are about to say.

Never finish a sentence with a preposition

This was always quite hard to obey. Prepositions are all those little words that aren't anything else, like up, of, to, in and so on. There are times when the only way to avoid putting one of them at the end of a sentence involves twisting the sentence self-consciously around until it becomes harder to follow.

There is a story (no doubt apocryphal) about Winston Churchill's view of this rule. His secretary told him he should rephrase a sentence because he had finished it with a preposition, and he supposedly replied: 'There are some things up with which I will not put!'

Never split an infinitive

Apart from anything else, who on earth can recognize a split infinitive these days? People over 60 and creeps, that's all (unless *you* can, in which case there are also some very clever people who understand them). The most famous modern example of a split infinitive is in the title sequence of *Star Trek* where the voiceover says: 'To boldly go ...' If it's good enough for the Starship *Enterprise*, it's good enough for us.

for next time

Rather than check through your proposal several times for grammatical and spelling errors, how much nicer to get it right first time. If you write a lot of proposals or reports, it's worth teaching yourself to write more correct English.

Don't push it: just pick one or two stumbling blocks at a time and learn the right way to do it, starting with the guidelines in this chapter. Then practise (that's practise with an 's', of course). Once you've learnt it confidently, move on to the next weak point and strengthen that, too.

You might like a small reference library to help you with this. I can thoroughly recommend the following to keep on your shelf:

- a dictionary
- a thesaurus (which gives groups of words with very similar meanings – invaluable when you can't quite remember a particular word)
- *The Complete Plain Words*, Ernest Gowers, Oxford University Press
- *Fowler's Modern English Usage*, Oxford University Press

▶ *The Economist Style Guide*, The Economist Books Ltd
▶ *The Penguin Dictionary of Troublesome Words*, Penguin

It's difficult to overexaggerate the value of a small but good reference shelf like this. And if you're at all under-confident about your writing skills it will help you turn out high-quality writing. And don't worry if you think you're hopeless at writing clearly and following all the guidelines: English is a sod of a language and we all look things up from time to time.

If a split infinitive is good enough for the Starship Enterprise, it's good enough for us

6 presentation

Nearly there. You've written the whole proposal now, to the structure we outlined earlier, and you may be wondering what's left. The answer is: the look of the thing. It's the first thing your readers will notice, and the difference between a clear, attractive layout or a wodge of impenetrable text is going to have a big impact on their attitude to it. Poor presentation can even put them off reading it altogether.

Getting the layout right is a quick job (you'll be pleased to hear) in this age of word processors. You can add in the presentation features after you've completed the main text. You can also add any appendices you need at this stage. So this is a simple but crucial step in preparing your proposal.

LAYOUT

Not only does a well-laid-out proposal look more readable and inviting, it also gives the impression of being more organized than one which is badly presented. So what are the features you need to incorporate to give your proposal the right look? A key rule here is don't worry how many pages it covers – it's better to have an eight-page proposal with lots of space and white page showing through than to cram the same material into four pages. Here are the best ways to improve your layout; use it as a checklist:

- Double space your proposal.
- Leave generous margins, and align the right-hand margin.
- Use plenty of headings and sub-headings: they give readers big clues at a glance, and help them to find any specific information they are looking for.
- Use plenty of paragraphs – a fresh one for each fresh thought, idea or concept.
- Use lists wherever you can – they are easier to follow than solid text when you are listing ideas, items or options. Give them bullet points, numbers, icons or whatever you choose to mark them.
- Summarise main sections briefly if it will help clarity: 'So those are our four key options ...' followed by a list, for example.
- You can give each paragraph or headed section a number if you wish, but don't get too complicated. It just confuses people if you number a paragraph 2.1.1.
- Put the odd point or piece of information in a box if you think this will help clarity – but don't overuse the feature.

PLAIN AND SIMPLE

Just because your word processor offers you 74 different fonts, this is not the time to play with them. Stick to one plain font, with perhaps one other for headings. You don't want to confuse your readers, or distract from the substance of your proposal.

APPENDICES

We've established, of course, that you need to back up all your arguments with hard facts. But if there are lots of them, you don't want to clutter your proposal with endless tables and charts. So put the key facts in the proposal and move the supporting data to the appendices. That way, those who want to can read it, and those who don't can avoid it altogether.

Technical information in particular is generally best moved to an appendix. Just make sure you direct readers to the appendix at the relevant point in the proposal. By the way, don't feel that if your proposal has no appendices that you have somehow failed. There's no point in including them for the sake of it, just because it looks more grown up to have an appendix.

LOOKING AHEAD

If you are including information in your proposal which is likely to be updated later, putting it in an appendix makes it easy to swap with the new data when the time comes.

LENGTH

It's worth mentioning length, because many people simply haven't a clue how long their proposal should be. You might feel that a long proposal will look more impressive, and as if you have worked harder, but in fact the reverse is often the case. How do you feel about the reports and proposals that land on your desk? With your busy schedule you probably like them to be as brief as possible.

Well, you're no different from your readers. They are equally busy, and they want quality, not quantity. Especially not quantity. That's why putting non-essential data in an appendix is such a good idea. So make sure you include everything necessary, but otherwise keep your proposal down to a few pages. Two or three pages is plenty if that covers everything.

The Duke of Wellington once sent a message to the War Office saying, 'I apologize for the length of these despatches but I did not have time to make them shorter.' You may be up against the clock right now, but you should still make sure your proposal is no longer than necessary.

for next time

Arranging the presentation of your proposal isn't a long task, but you might find in future that you would like to experiment with types of bullet points, heading styles and so on. Please do so. But whatever you do, make sure the end result stays clear and simple.

Unless you're a designer touting for work, you should let the content of your proposal be the star of the show, not the cosmetics.

Unless you're a designer touting for work, you should let the content of your proposal be the star of the show, not the cosmetics

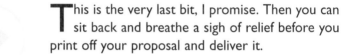

7 topping and tailing

This is the very last bit, I promise. Then you can sit back and breathe a sigh of relief before you print off your proposal and deliver it.

There are lots of little bits and pieces which you need to add to your proposal, many of them as a kind of garnish that makes the proposal look really impressive and helps the reader through it, too. They are the finishing touches. You won't need all of them every time – sometimes you will use very few of them – but you need to know what they are. And you need to add them last of all.

This book, like any book, has a title page, information about publishers and copyright, a contents page and so on. Some books also have a bibliography, or a useful addresses section. So what we're talking about is the proposal version of this packaging.

REGULAR FEATURES

We'll start with the features just about every proposal should include:

-  title page with title and author

- contents page (if the proposal is more than four pages including any appendices)

- the objective – here it is again. You may need to reword it slightly, but state it below the title, or at the start of the proposal somewhere

- summary (we'll look at this in a moment)

- page numbers.

OCCASIONAL FEATURES

And now for the features that you will sometimes need to include. These can all go at the back, although you might prefer to put the acknowledgements at the front:

- acknowledgements – of other people who have helped or contributed

- appendices

- glossary (if you have had to use jargon your readers might not understand)

- bibliography

- references – referring to the sources you've used boosts your credibility so list interviews, catalogues, books, reports, media sources, trade associations or anything else you think will convince or impress

- further addresses.

The finishing touches are a kind of garnish that makes the proposal look really impressive

Summary

Unless your report is extremely brief, some of your readers may not have time to read it all. Even if they do, they may want to recap it later without having to read the whole thing again. What they need is a summary. Not a summary in the sense of a conclusion, but a précis or résumé that briefly summarizes the report or proposal.

Every report or proposal that runs to more than three or four pages should have a summary at the beginning, straight after the contents page. So what should you put in it? If you think about it, it's quite simple. If this is the only part of the report that some of your readers will see, you want to include everything. Only shorter.

The summary should be a miniature version of the report or proposal, complete in itself, so the key facts are clear to anyone who reads it, even if they read nothing else. This being the case, it

thinking smart

UNDER COVER

Always put your proposal into some kind of report folder (through which the title shows) before presenting it. It looks smart, is easier to find among a pile of papers, and will protect it from coffee rings and other damage.

should obviously follow the same structure as the full version:

- ▷ **position**
- ▷ **problem**
- ▷ **possibilities (if they apply)**
- ▷ **proposal.**

thinkingfast

FIRST THINGS LAST

It is far more sensible and much quicker to write the summary *after* you've written the main body of the document. You've already covered the ground by then, and it's just a matter of pulling out the most central information.

for next time

If you are in a real rush, you may have to miss out a few of these. Make sure you retain the essential ones, but you might need more time to include a full list of references, further addresses, bibliography and so on. When you have more time, however, you should include these if you can since they give your proposal more weight, and can answer specific questions for your reader (such as, 'Where on earth has Jo dragged up these statistics from?').

Every report or proposal that runs to more than three or four pages should have a summary at the beginning

proposal in an evening

If you feel panicky, read the last bit of the book: Proposals in an hour. If that's possible, this should be a breeze. Begin by reading this book right through. It'll only take you an hour, so there's plenty of time.

One of your biggest drawbacks is going to be the difficulty of getting hold of the data you need to back up your proposal. If you already have them, great. If not, anything you can find out by phone needs doing first of all, before it gets too late. If you need to call colleagues and ask them to e-mail you facts and figures, do it now.

Other than that, writing a proposal at this kind of speed is all about knowing which stages in the process you can skip and still get away with it. So here are some suggestions for trimming down the time it takes to get this thing written.

- Keep the proposal as short as you possibly can without sacrificing any essential points. It has to be quicker to write three pages than to write eight. It won't be much quicker at the planning stage, but when it comes to physically writing the thing it will save you time.

- If the proposal is short enough (three to four pages maximum) you can skip the contents page and the summary page.

- Drag in any help you possibly can. Come on! There must be plenty of people out there who owe you favours. Get suggestions from colleagues about arguments to use, advice about what issues your readers consider important, talk them into digging out facts for you and, if you know anyone who can write good English and is on e-mail, get them to go through your draft proposal for you and e-mail it back corrected. Offer bottles of Scotch, tickets to Wimbledon, a go on your playstation – whatever will persuade them to help you out.

- Don't economize on time spent on presentation. First impressions are vital – especially if you don't want the reader to spot any economies you may have made elsewhere.

- Don't economize on facts either. If you can't find the data, don't include the argument. If it's essential, and you have to include it, dig out the data tomorrow morning as soon as you have delivered the proposal. That way, if anyone queries it, you'll at least be able to come back with the goods.

If it still looks neat, you may be able to copy or scan in data for appendices, rather than retype it. But be aware that this can contravene copyright law if you are using copyrighted material — even if it's only for internal circulation to a few people. Internal documents or copyright-free material, however, are fine.

If you follow these tips, you'll have plenty of time to prepare your proposal in an evening, even if it doesn't leave you the time or the energy to follow it with a slap-up meal and a couple of videos. It may, however, persuade you to try even harder when you write your next proposal to find more time in which to do it. But, for now, relax and stay cool. People have written proposals in less time than this *and* come out looking smart and winning their case.

Your objective is the one thing you most need to give you clarity of purpose

proposal in an hour

Even by fast thinking standards you're pushing it a bit, aren't you? Write a proposal in an hour? Are you serious? OK, then. If you're serious enough about it, it can be done. Especially if you're used to working under time pressure – which I guess you must be to have arrived at this point.

So what can you do in an hour? Write a very short proposal. And actually, as long as everything is in there, a short proposal can be every bit as effective and impressive as a longer one. You'll just need to employ great clarity of thought:

1 You need to start by working out your objective (Chapter 1). No, it's not a waste of time. It's the one thing you most need to give you clarity of purpose.

2 Forget research. I presume you've got a pile of facts and data fairly readily to hand or you wouldn't be cutting things this fine. If you

haven't, it's too late anyway. Skip straight to the chapter about structure (Chapter 3), and fit what you need to say into this structure as succinctly as possible.

3 Now type it up on your word processor, if you haven't already done it as you went along.

4 Go through the proposal and look for any points which need explaining better (in which case see pages 59–60). Change any words you're not certain you are using correctly. And make sure your words, sentences and paragraphs are nice and short. Don't try to be clever with language.

5 Bang through the thing and correct your English, check your spelling and all that stuff. Twice. (I know you won't really do it twice but I have to say it, because we both know you ought to. When you're in a rush you make more mistakes than usual.)

6 Now tart up the layout, according to Chapter 6. It's OK, it's a really short chapter. Just checklists really.

7 Same goes for Chapter 7, all about topping and tailing. You're going to need a title page, which should include your objective. And don't forget to add page numbers.

8 And finally … don't make a habit of this. My blood pressure can't take it even if yours can.

It is far more sensible and much quicker to write the summary *after* you've written the main body of the document